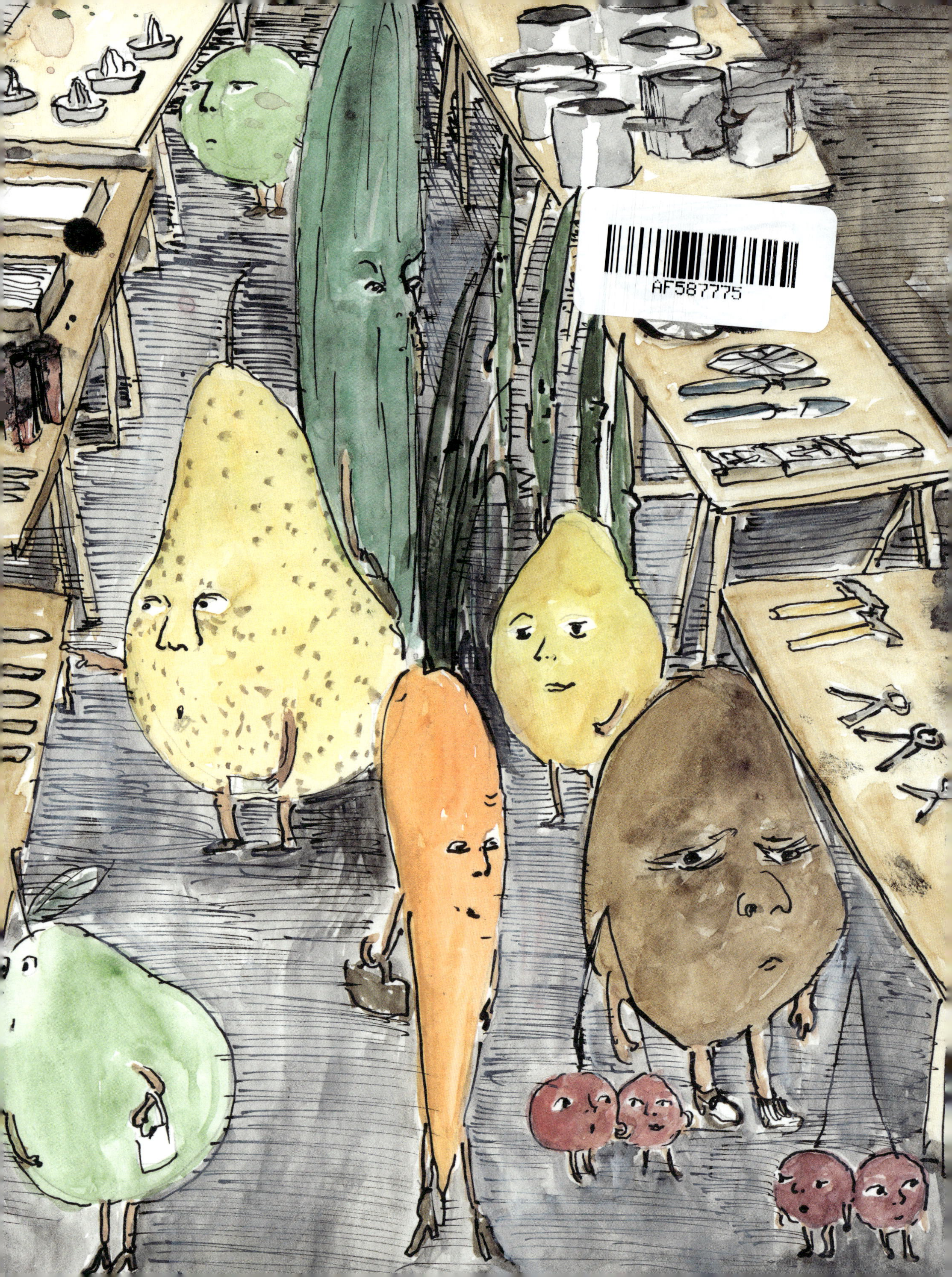

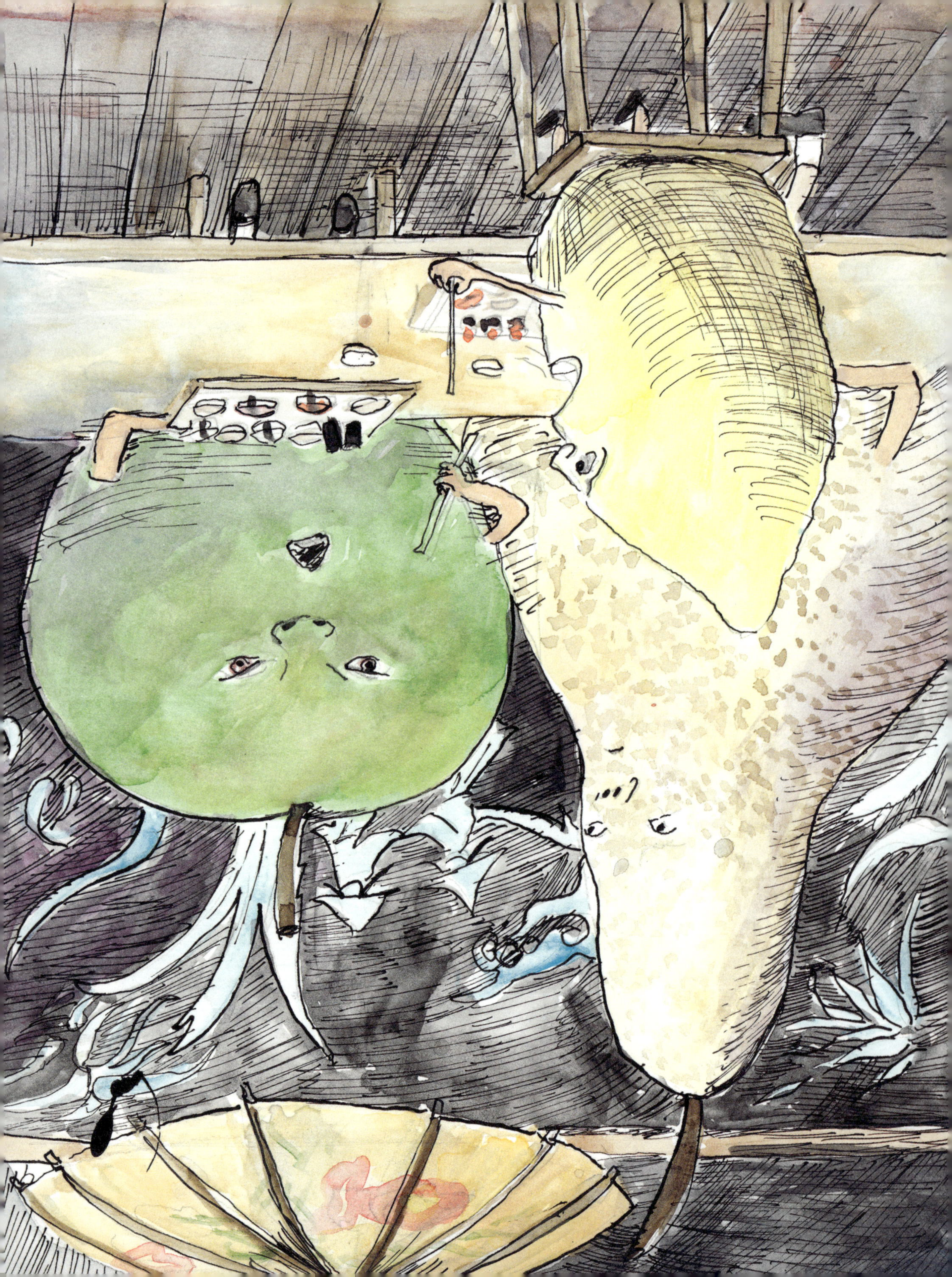

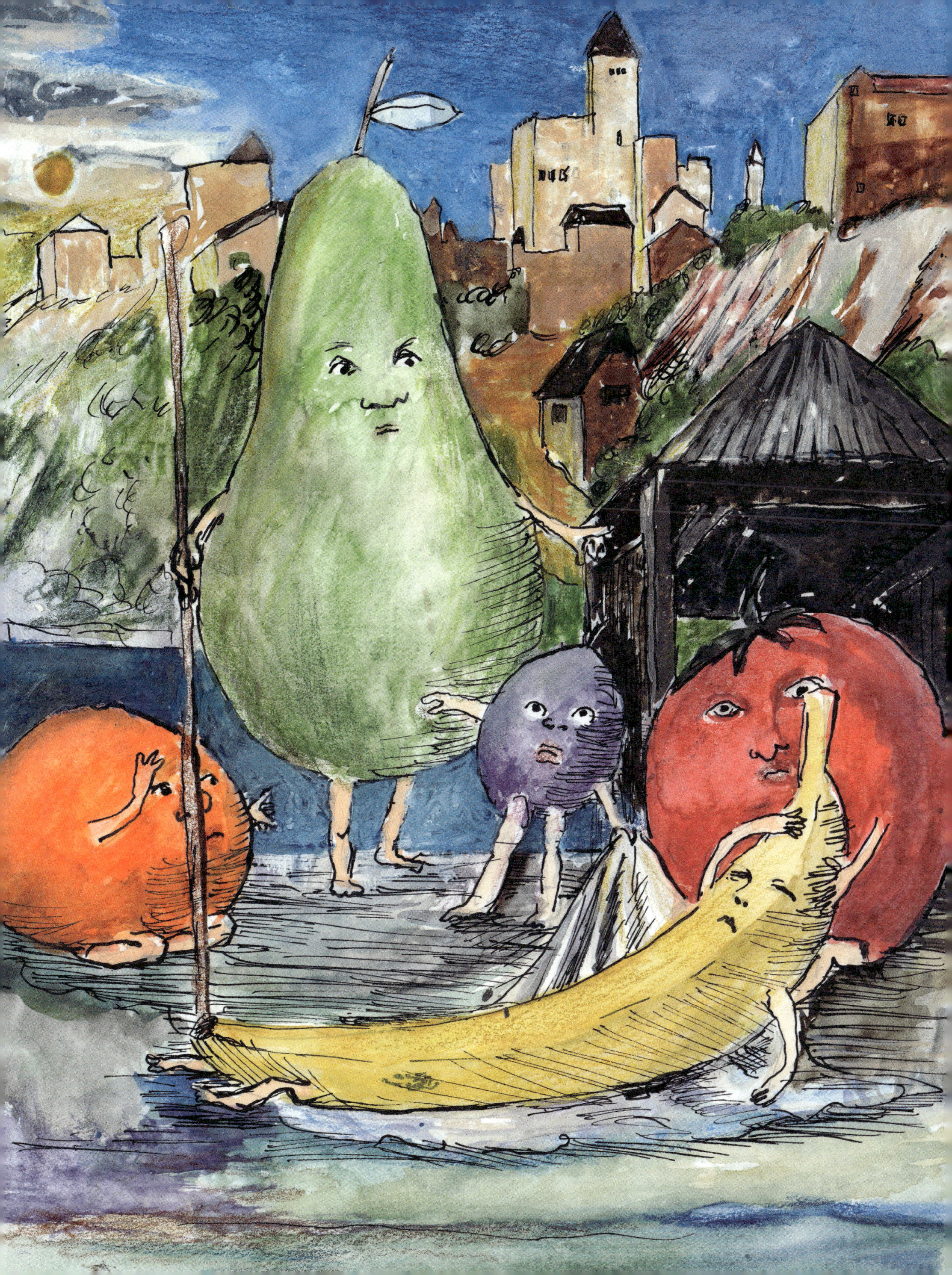

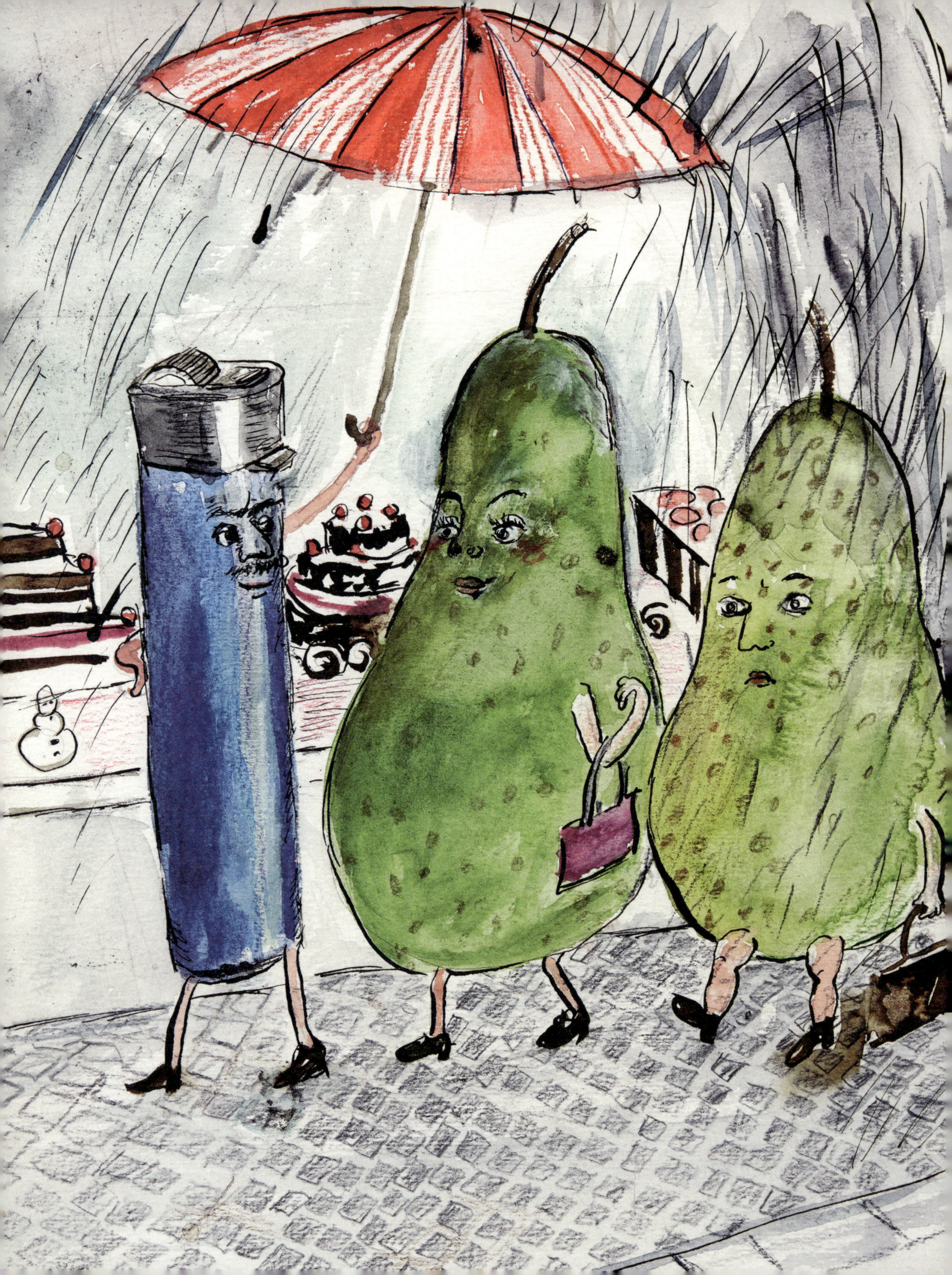

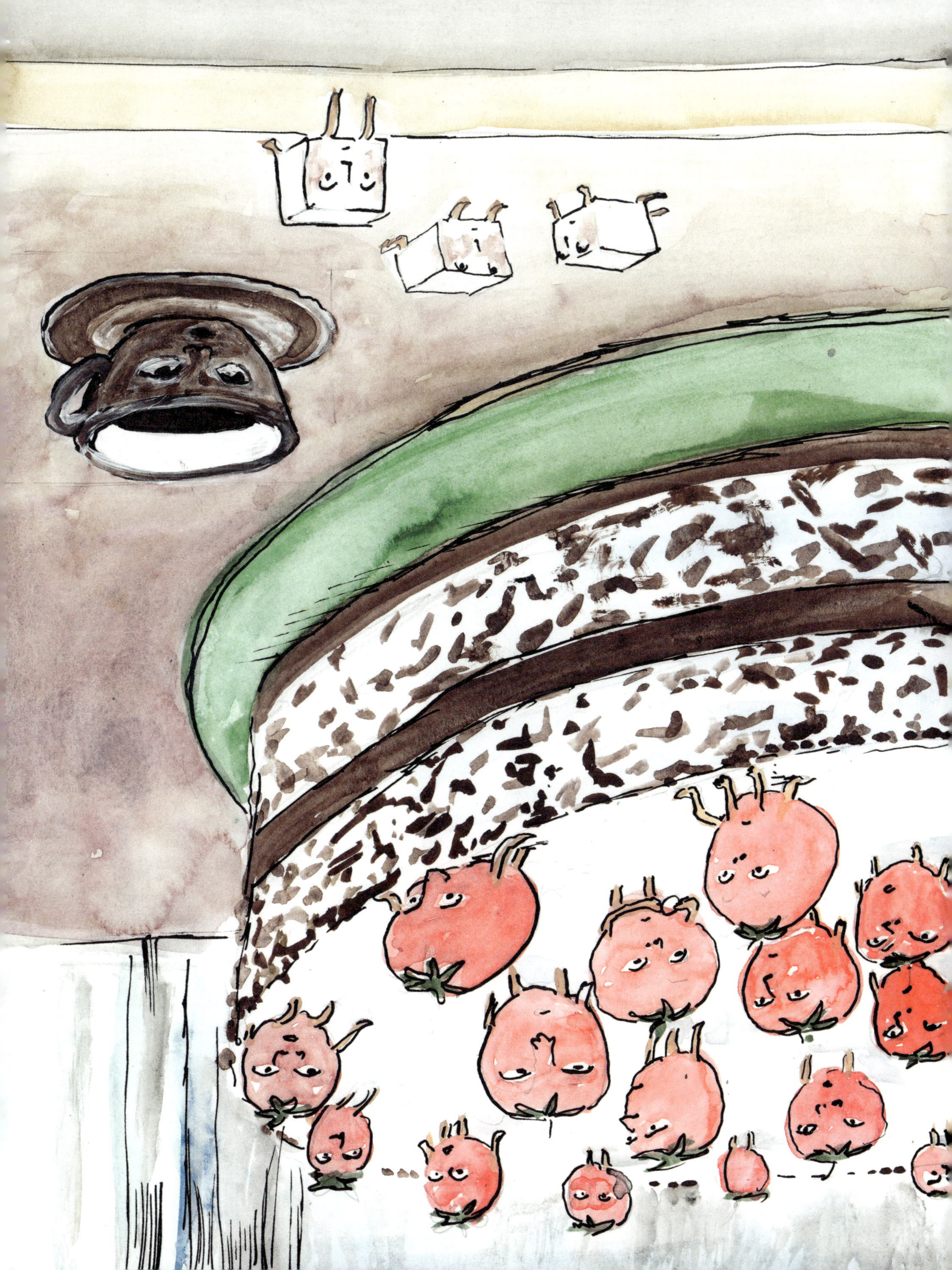

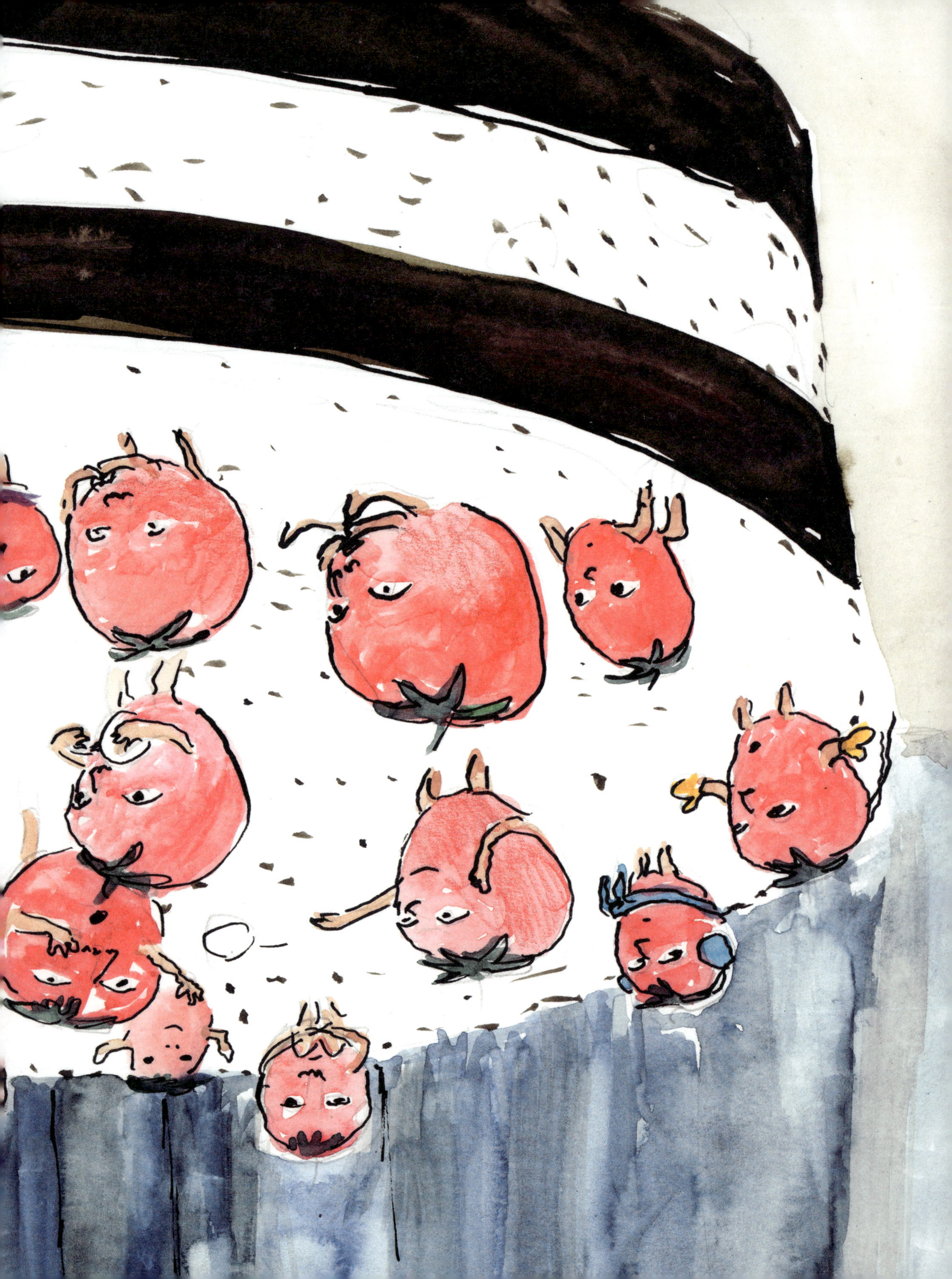

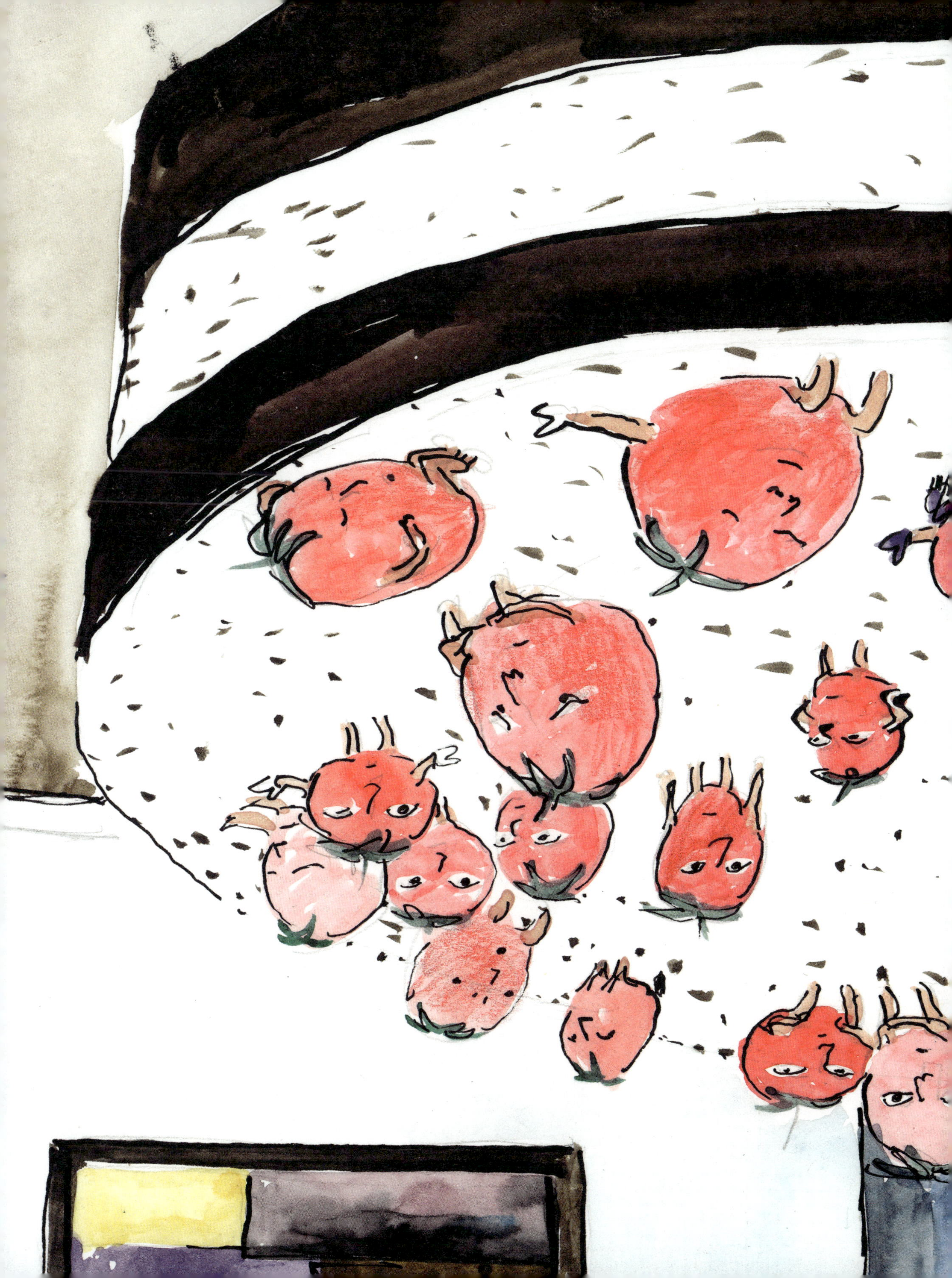

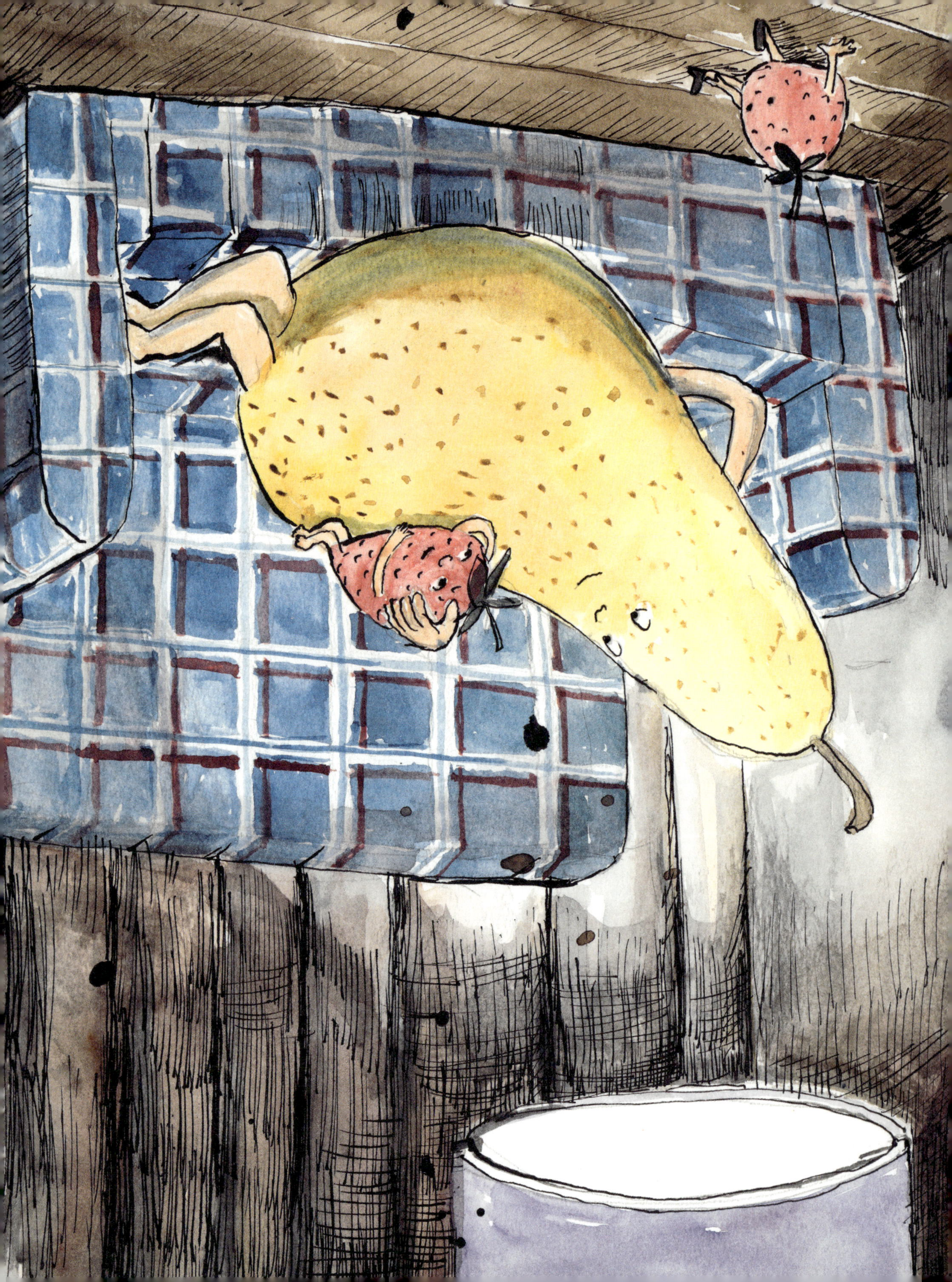

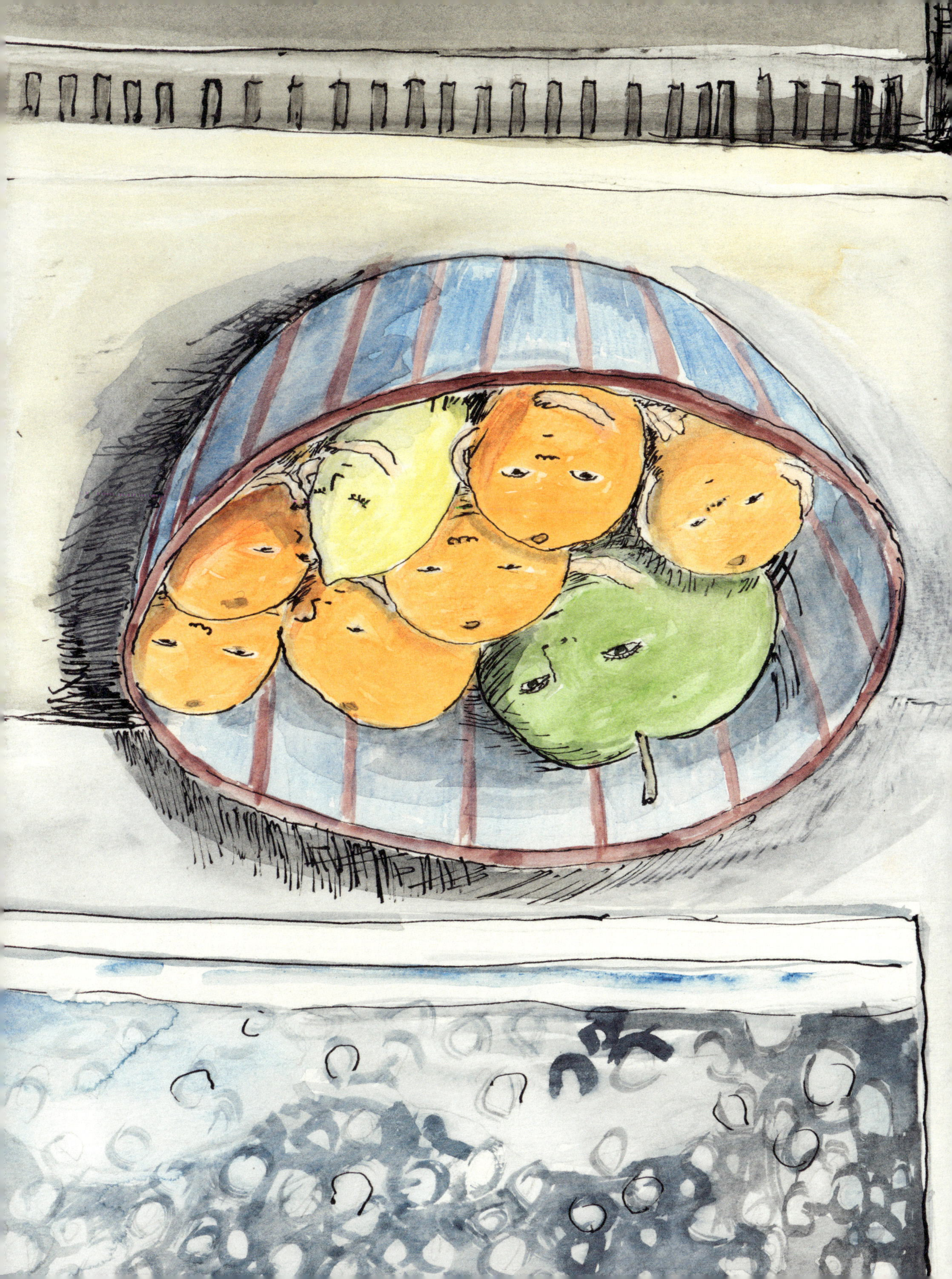

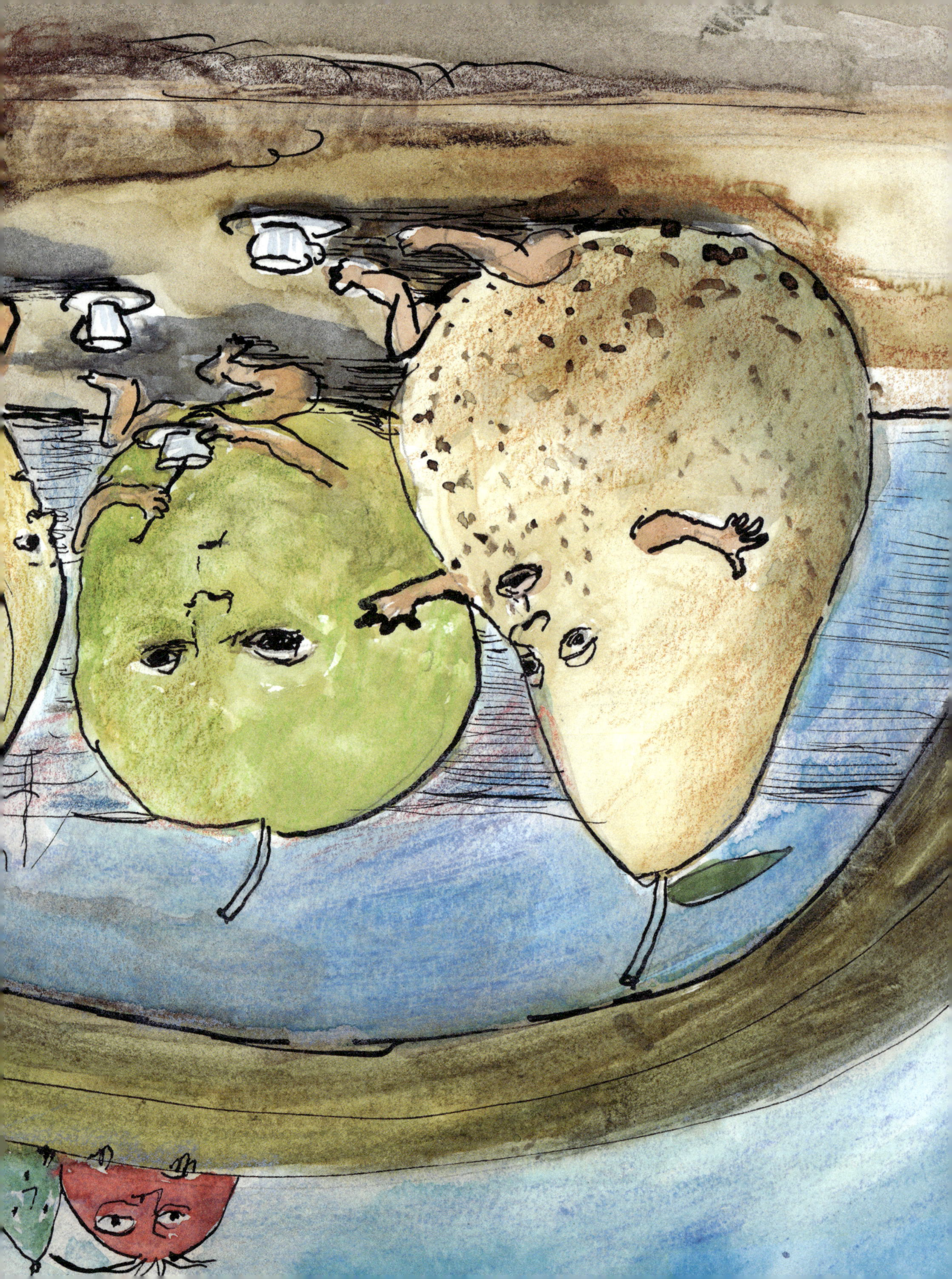

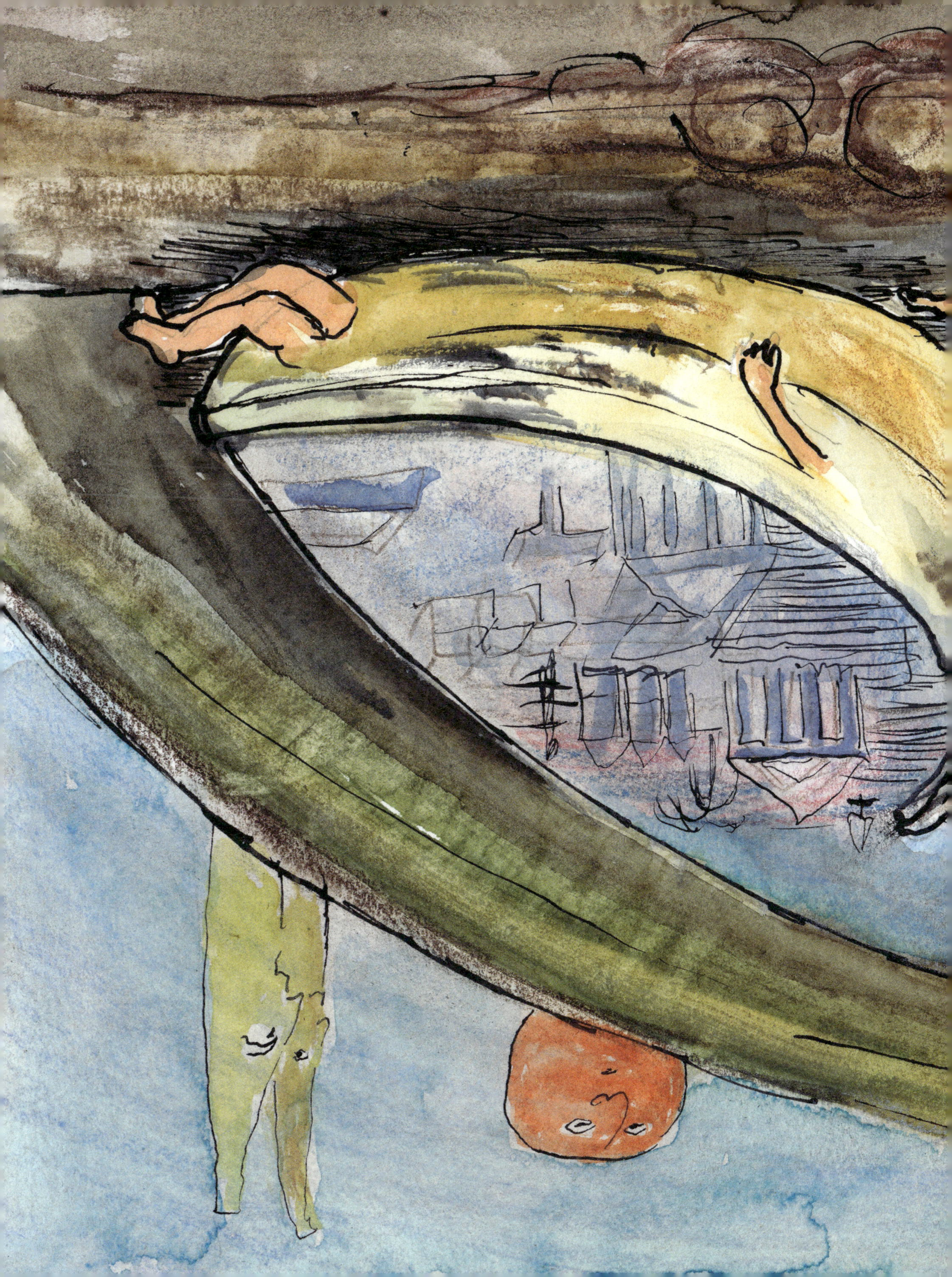

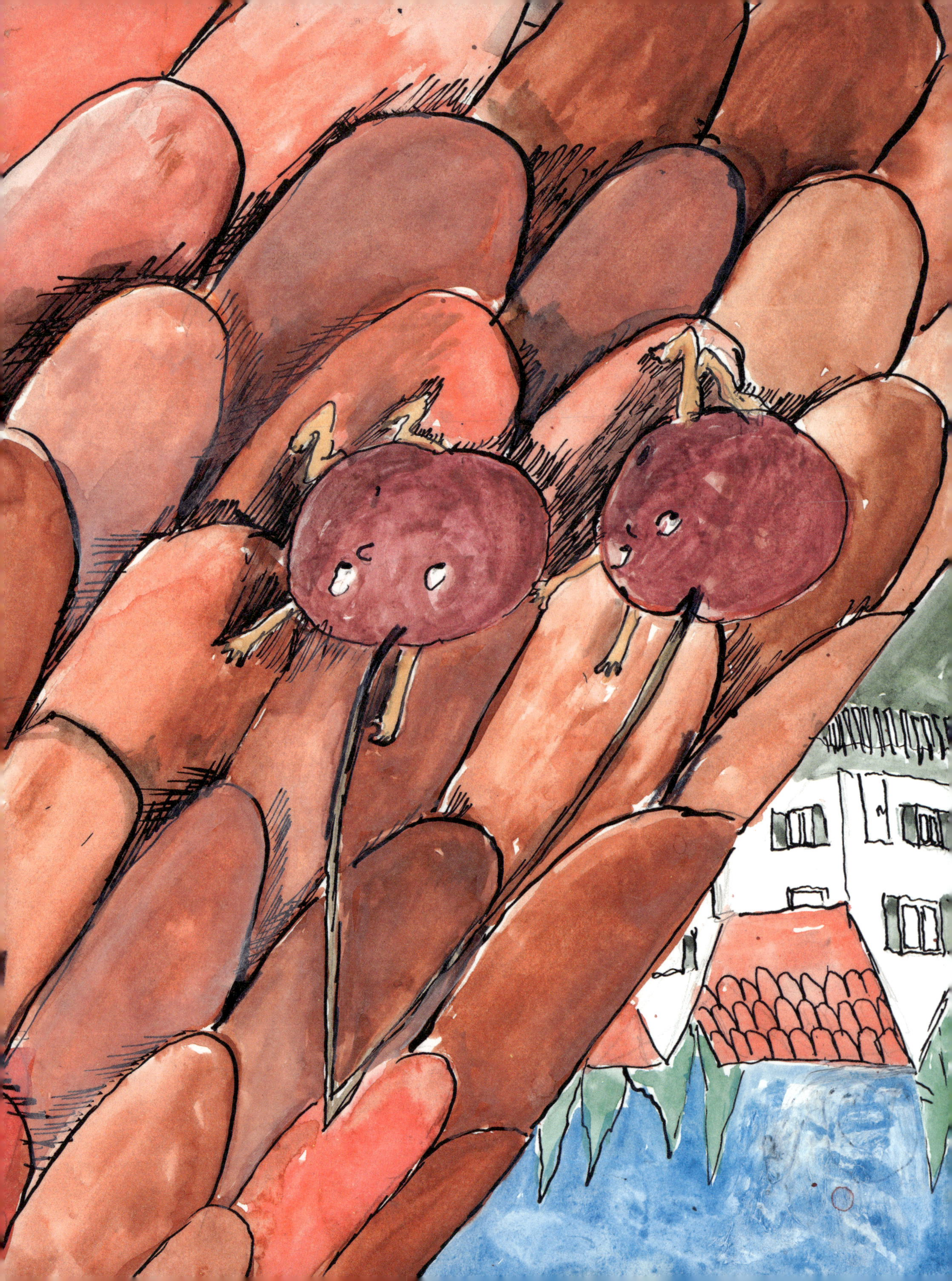

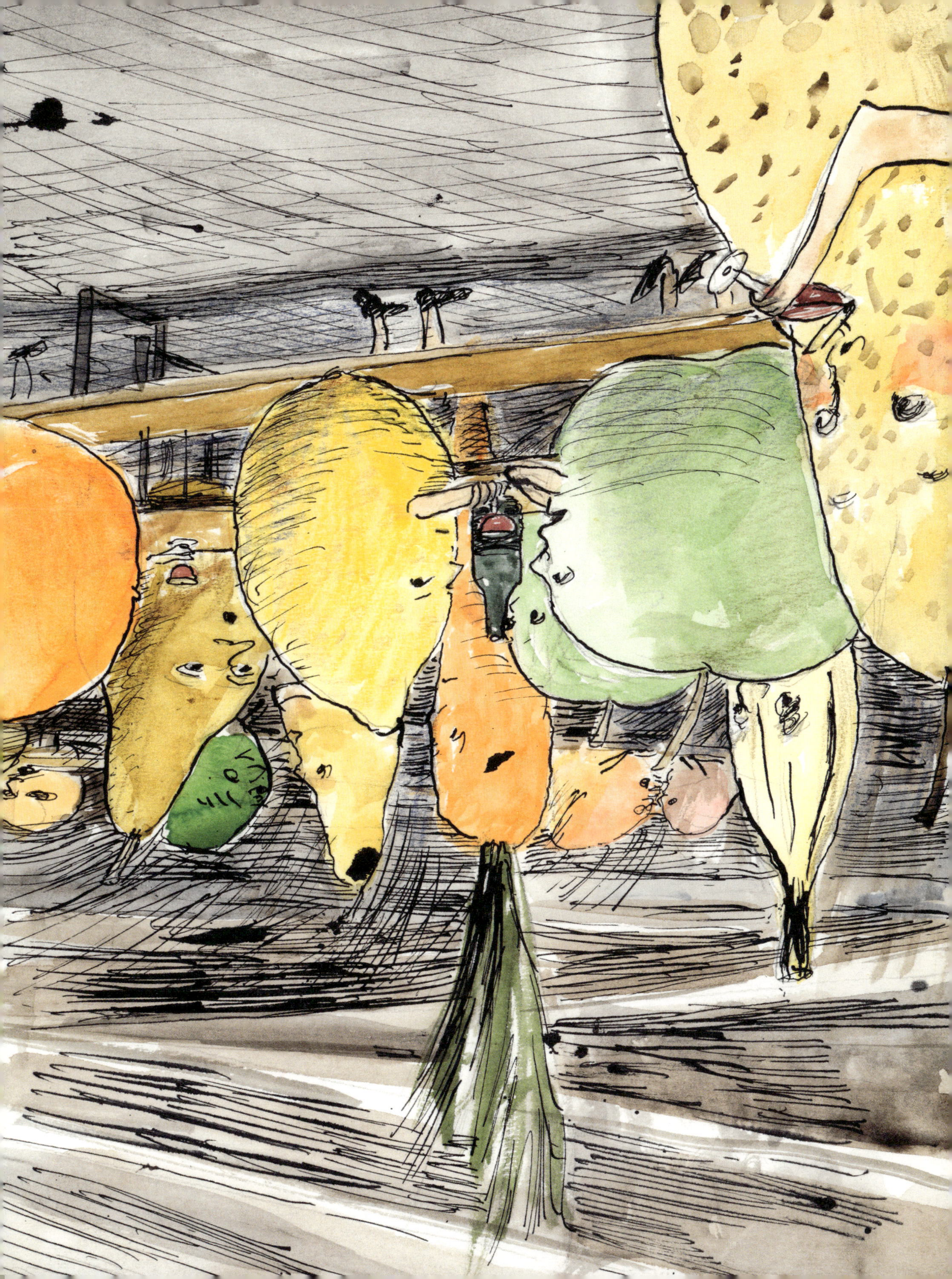

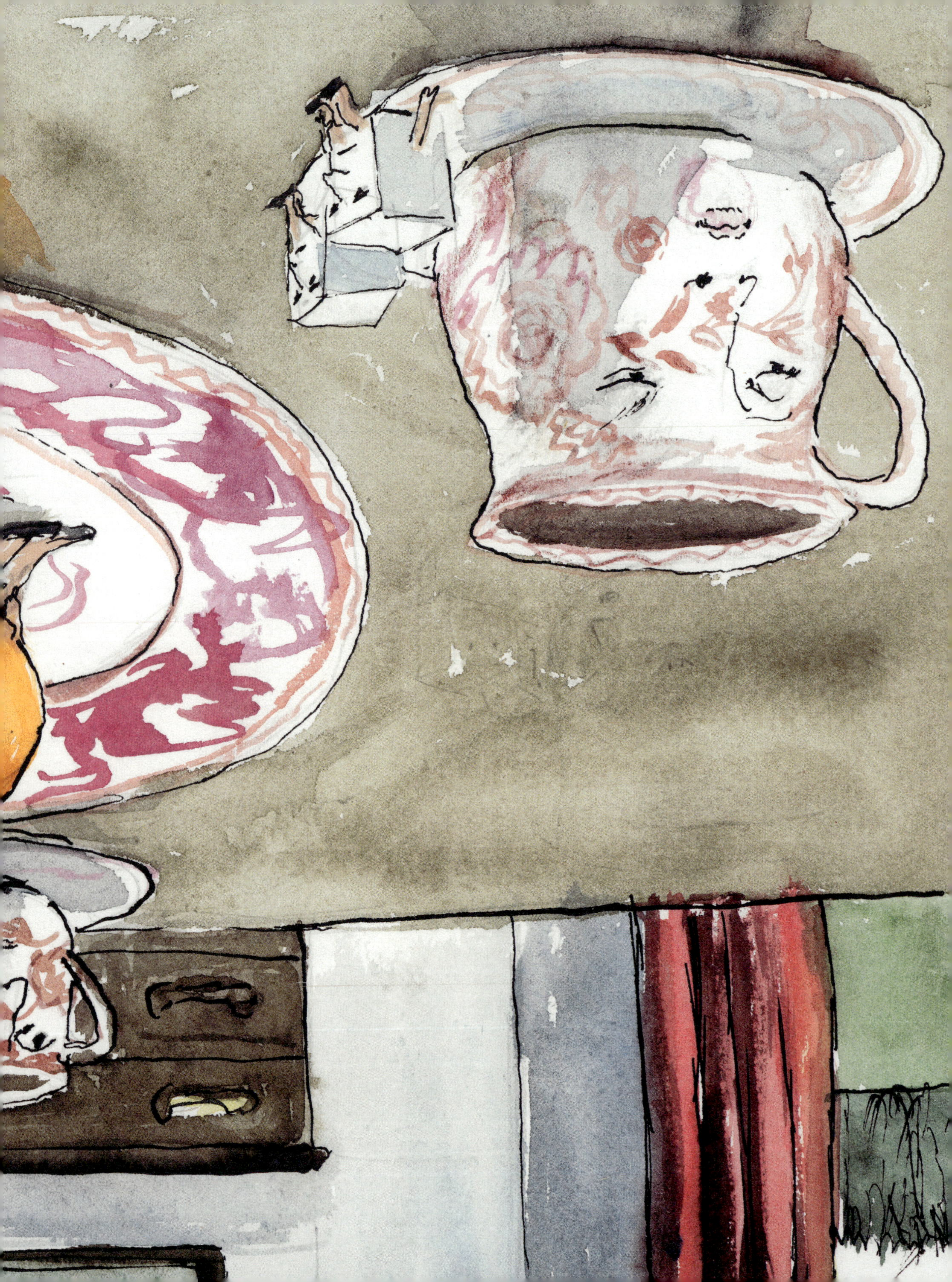

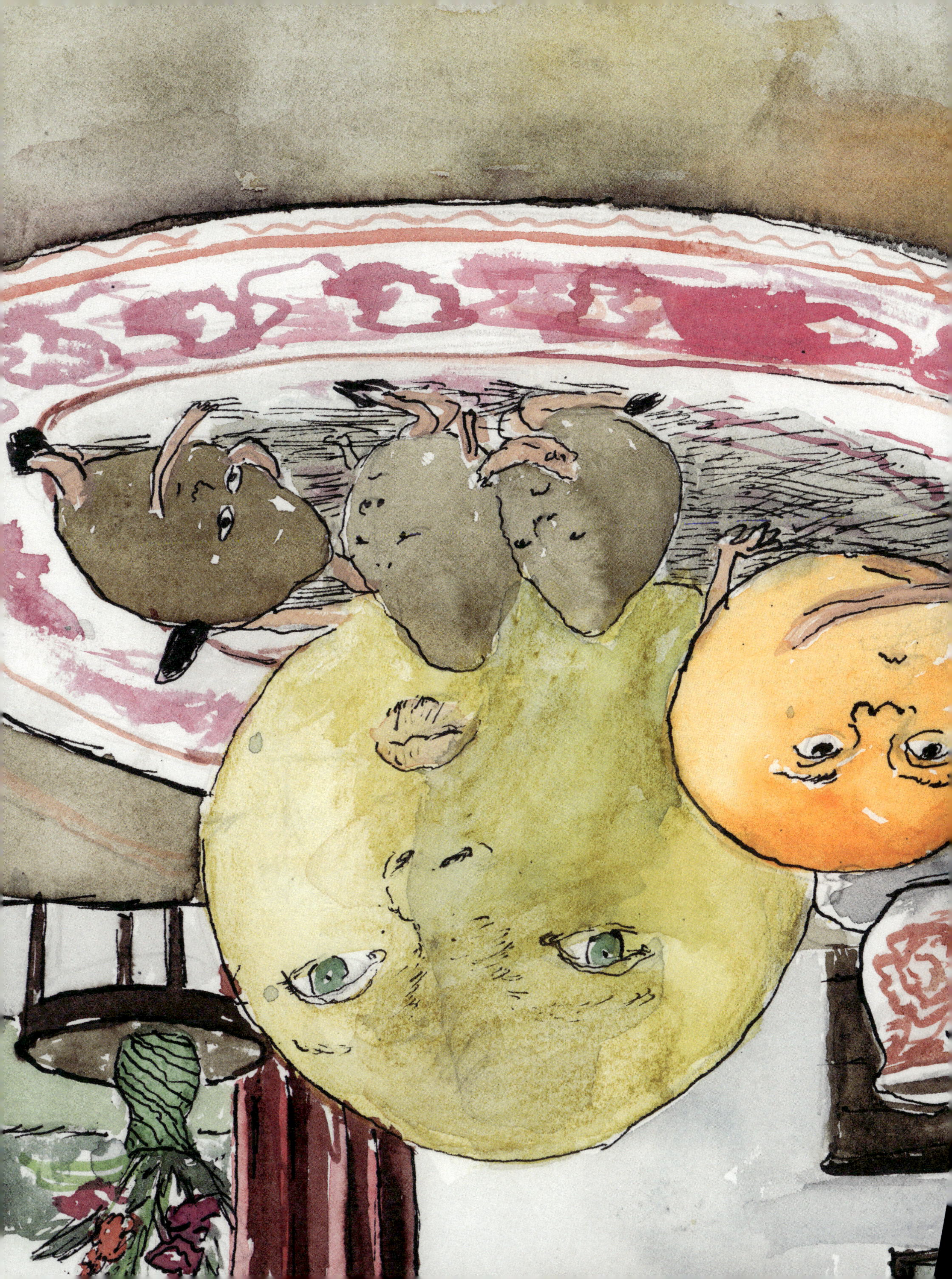

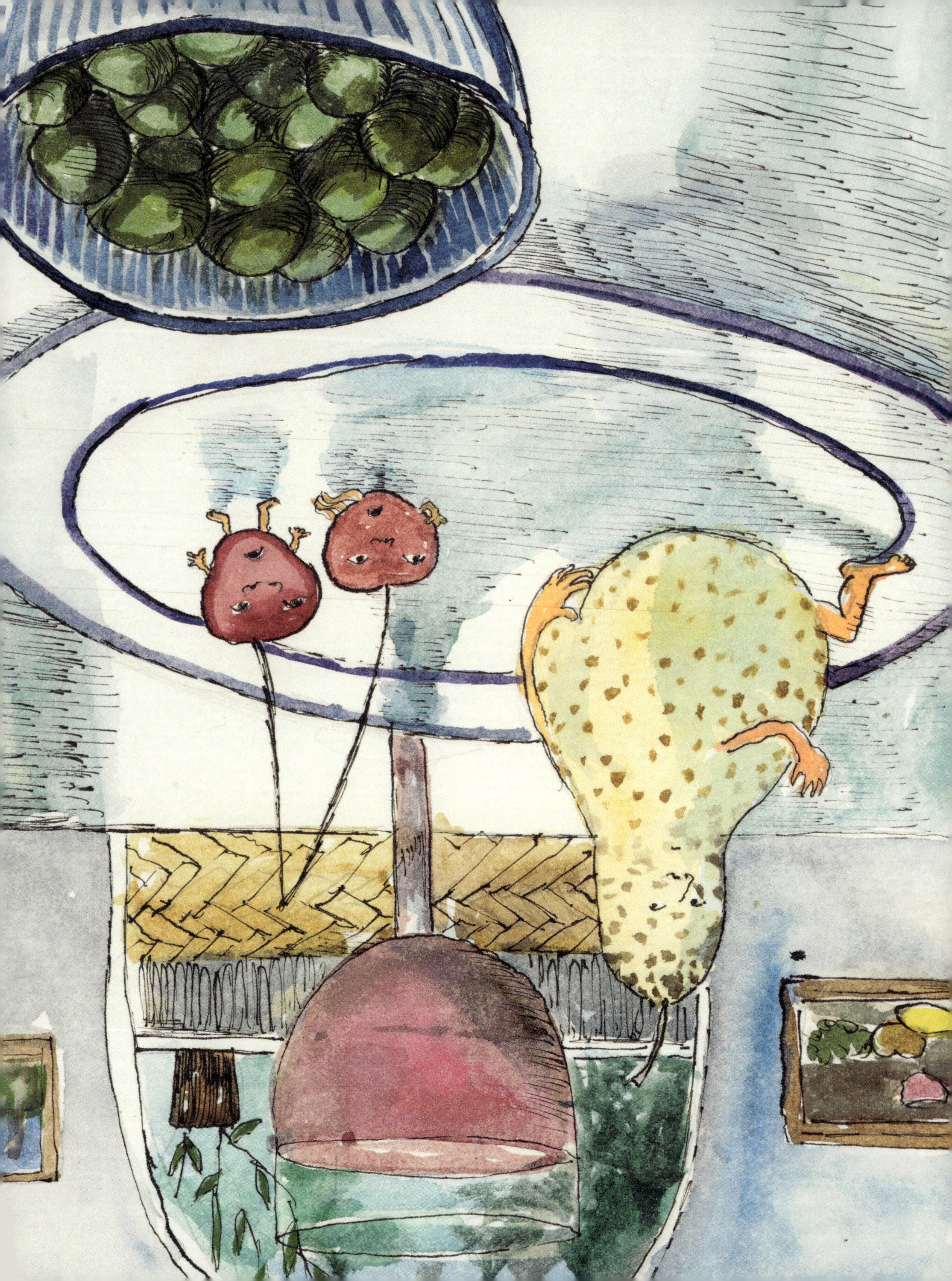

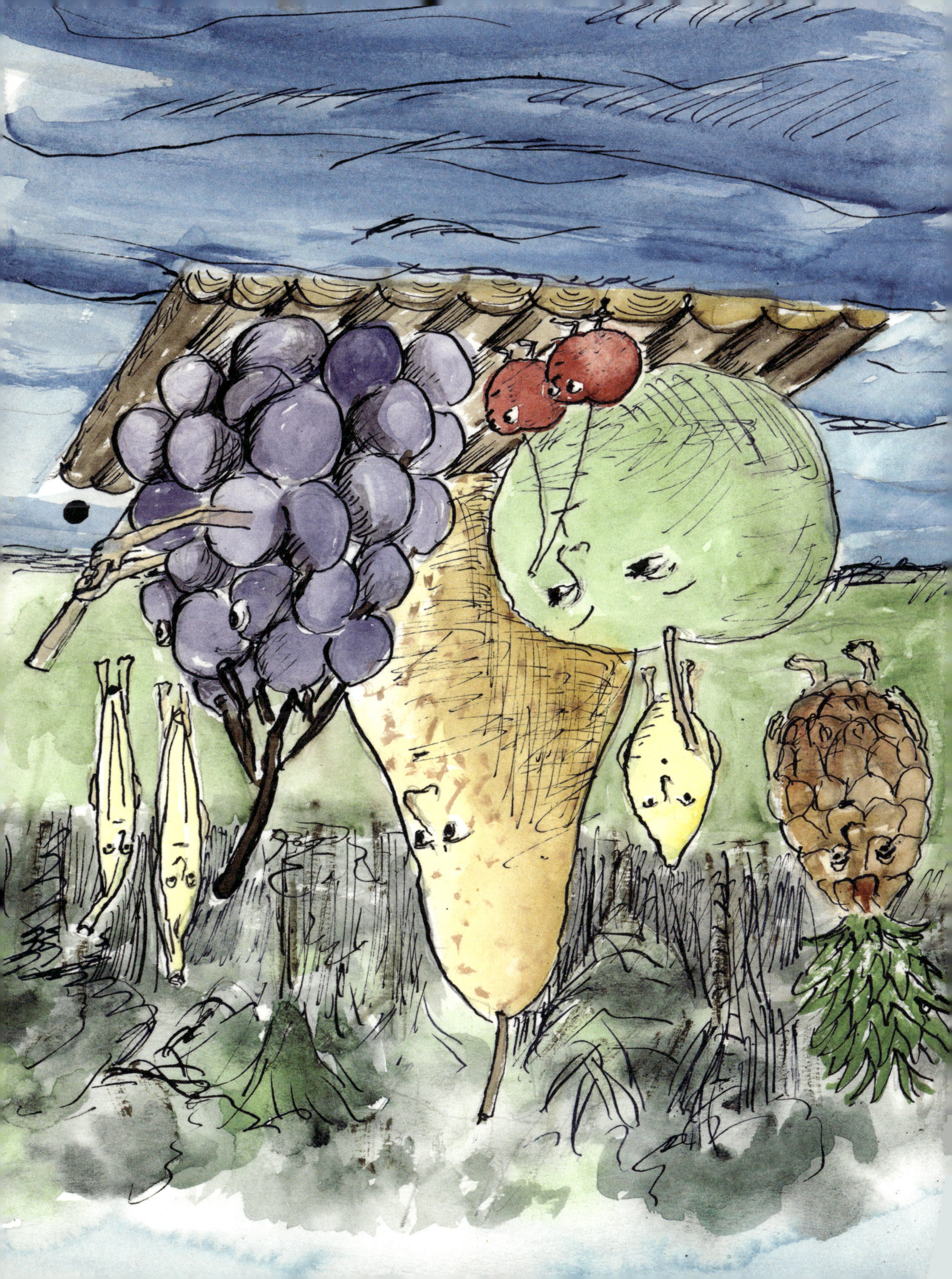

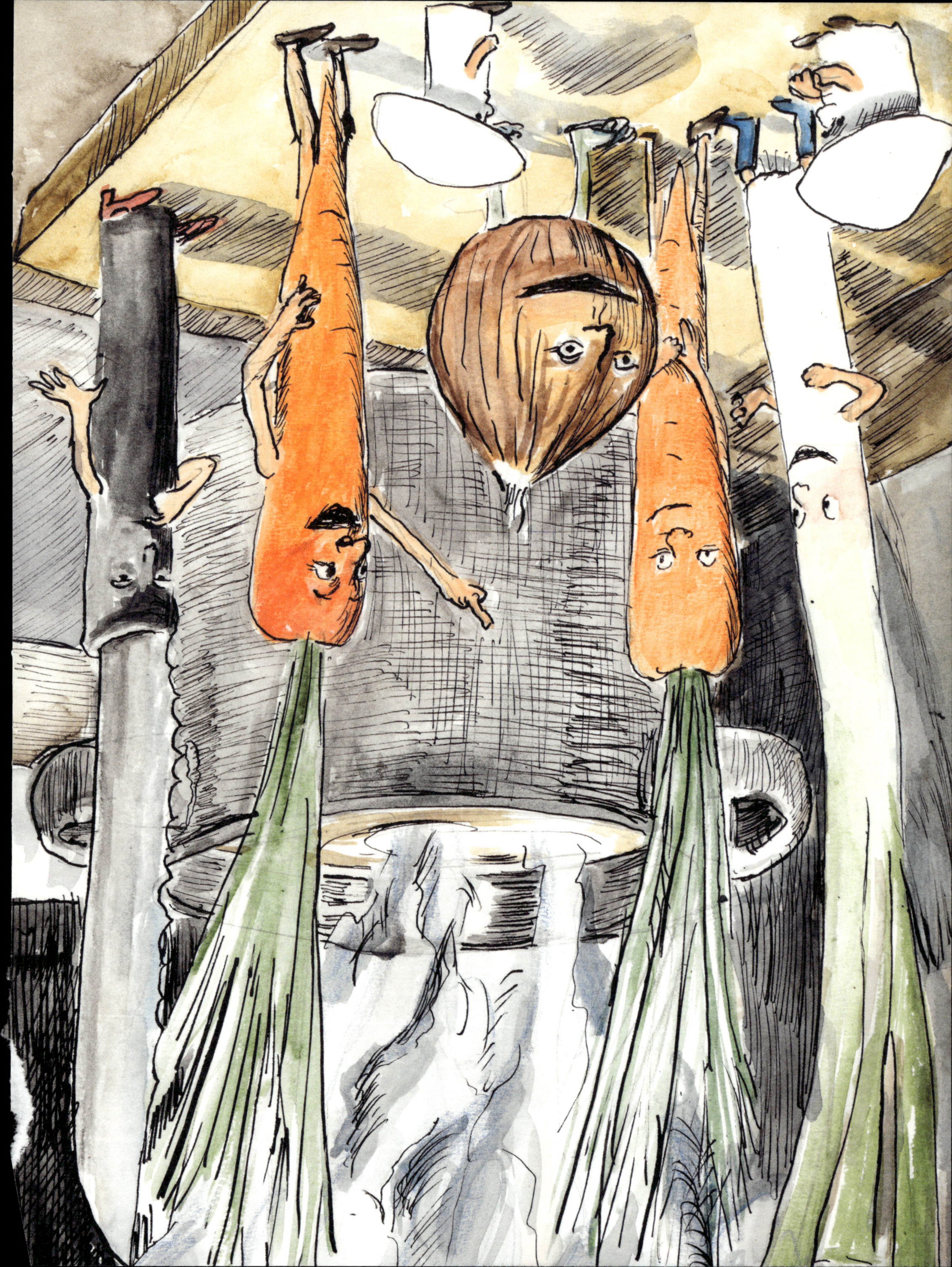

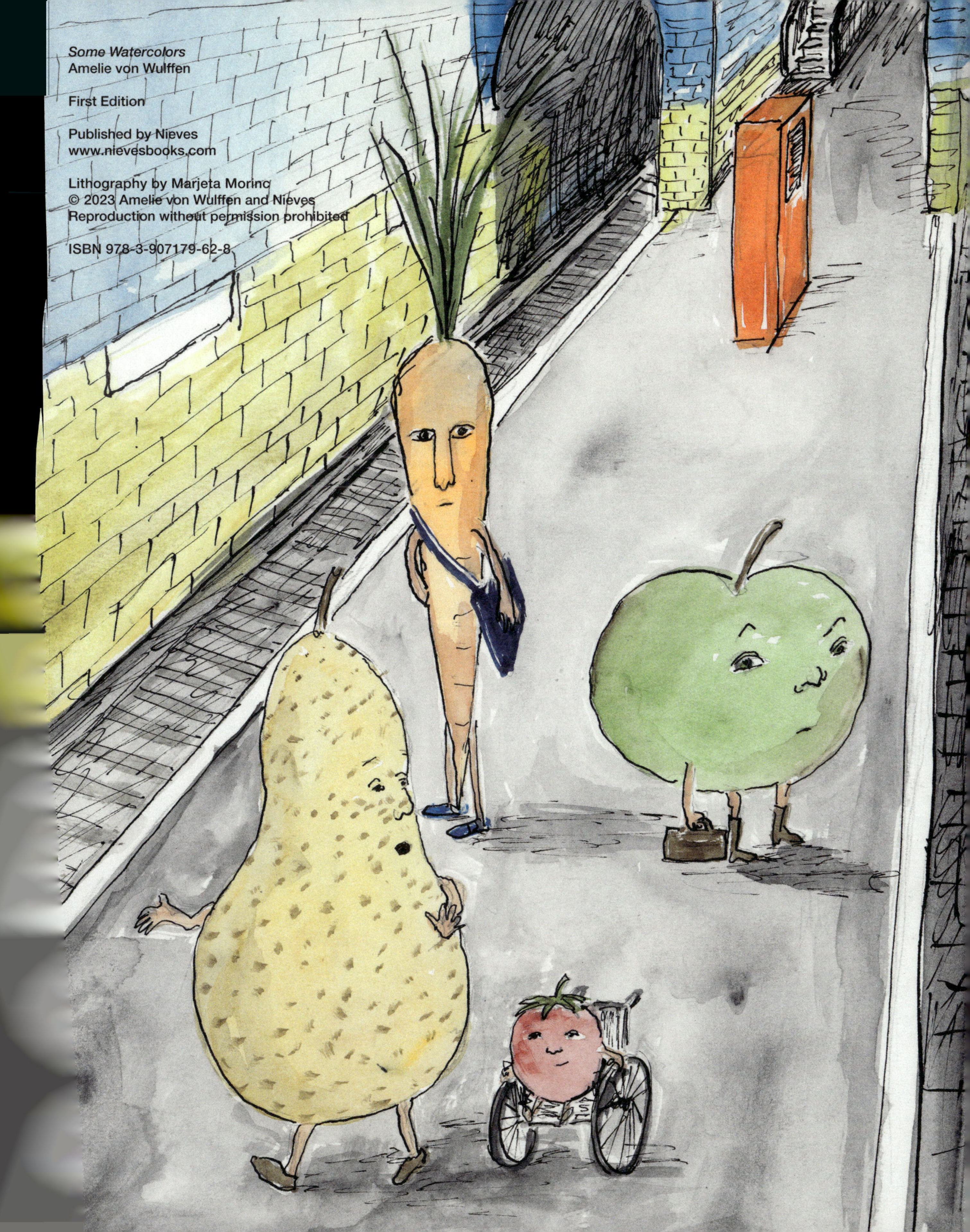

Some Watercolors
Amelie von Wulffen

First Edition

Published by Nieves
www.nievesbooks.com

Lithography by Marjeta Morinc

ISBN 978-3-907179-62-8

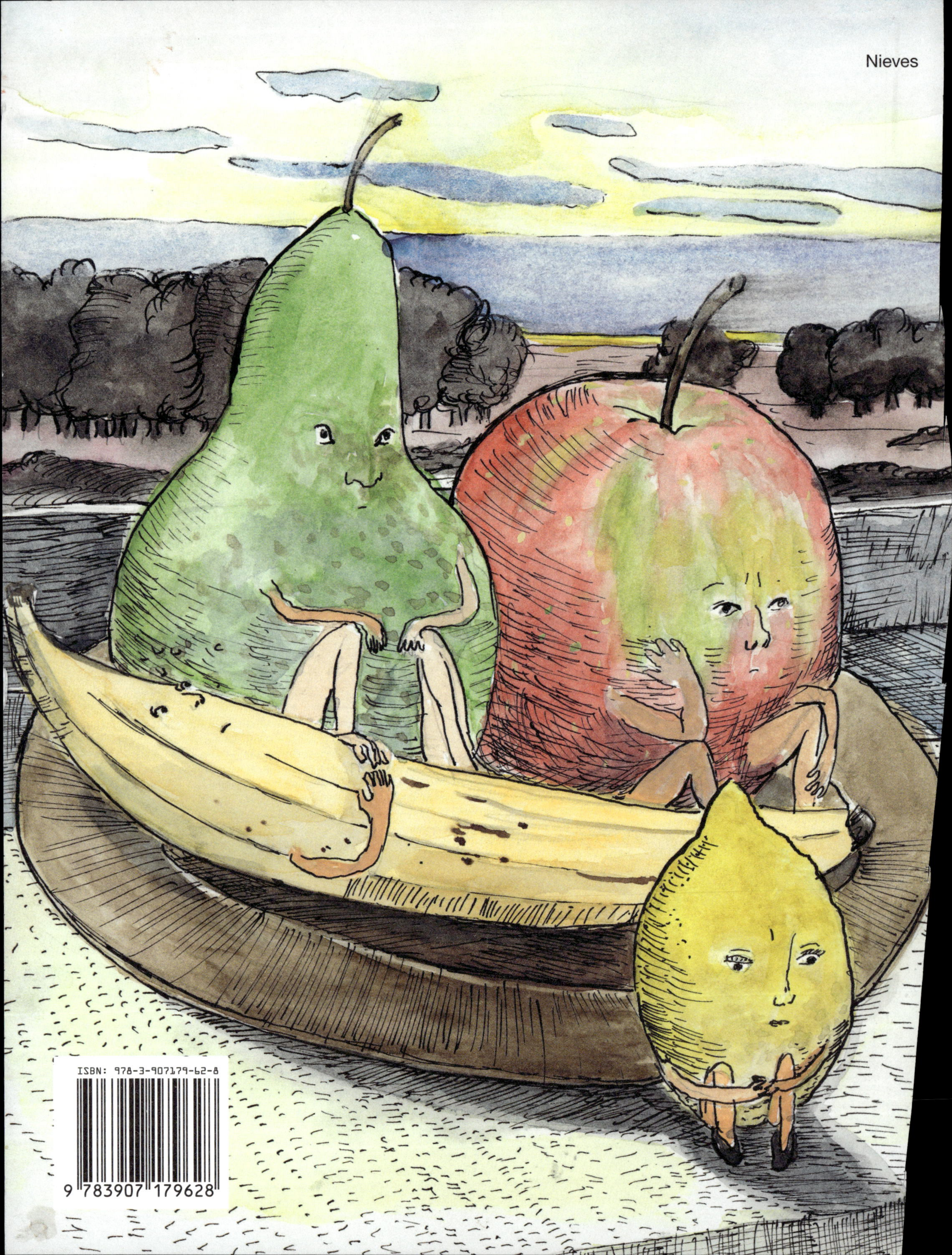

ISBN: 978-3-907179-62-8
9 783907 179628